You Know What Happened to Thought?
A Poetry Compilation

MEGHAN VICTORIA

You Know What Happened to Thought?

A Poetry Compilation

Meghan Victoria

Table of Contents

You Know What Happened to Thought?

A Poetry Compilation

Meghan Victoria

You Know What Happened to Thought?

A Poetry Compilation

Meghan Victoria

..my rock
my roll
forget me not
as we grow old.

Not Quite Left (2002)

I feel misplaced like I do not belong
I feel like I'm somewhere
but that somewhere is wrong
I feel like a toy on the wrong shelf
or a blade of grass
standing all by itself

I can't really tell my left from my right
I can't separate simple colors
like black from white..
I hear the wind calling my name back home
but here I can't tell
which way the wind has blown. End.

Oak Street Music

I see skies of blue
and a small brook that runs through
neighborhood gardens
sprouting life so new
A world amidst green
Apartments dropped into trees
the children, like clockwork,
disappear like the leaves..
They don't run in circles
they cycle right angles
cutting the corners
off the concrete rectangles..
And they loved those bricks that
encompassed their lives,
and the warmth in their homes
when the sun's on their side..
We used to dance, my sister and I..
where the cigarette smoke gathered in the sunlight
And our father would turn on his old stereo
that he bought
when our mom and he got
their first home..
He was cold but allowed us a glimpse at his soul
when he showed off
what he thought
was true rock n roll..
He fought for so long,
but we still got older
and shouldered the verses each insert unfolded..
Bold and soft-spoken.. we each took a token
a piece of reprieve from a record so broken
Here we go hoping.. and focused on showing him
all that we learned from the music we'd stolen. End.

Four Eyes

Unjustly enriched
and alcohol dipped
moronic with wit..
and selfishly stitched..
as he sits with the bricks
he denies being his
while he picks apart
all of the things that I think. End.

Blame the Rain (2005)

I watch the rain
streaming down my window
and I can't help but think,
if I were to stand outside
no one could see me cry..
'cause I'll just blame the rain..

and I watch the rain
create a puddle out my door..
and while I wander through it
I wonder why
it isn't sunny anymore

When I'm in the rain
I need no umbrella..
It can't protect me from the cold..
Since there is no rain
I look up to the clouds
and I ask them to shower on my fears
and I ask them to hide my many tears..
'cause I'll just blame the rain. End.

Empty (2006)

The glass is so half empty tonight
and with all my craziest motions,
I never saw tears run so dry..
.. like I really lack those emotions..
Wearing shades on cloudy days
I sure could use the rain..
I feel the drought in many ways..
.. as I cower from such pain..
My tears are tight.. yet so unused
My heart truly is broken..
Your memory is my new muse..
.. those words are barely spoken..
But I can stand up straight onward..
and stare on with this view,
because falling apart is not what I intend..
but I hope you sleep restfully soon. End.

Rattle Can

I'm running down the tracks
Rattle can, red stain
sneakers, spare change
Life's sure changing fast

I watched the time tick in his hands
and felt him grant enough to me
to empty several cans

miles from my home
I stand, and know
that no one is looking for me,
as my exhaled smoke dances free
beneath the streetlight glow
for just a moment, I enjoy the show

then pull my cap over my ears
drop the bag
pull on my mask
and raise my hand to throw one last,
before we switch our gears..

they promised me they'd bring me back out here
I told them that I couldn't handle anything sincere

Rattle can, red stain
sneakers, spare change
Damn, that sun sure rises fast
when the day begins to break. End.

Tag

Her silence looks like weakness
.. knees pulled tight up to her chest
she listens to these strangers speak,
absorbing their demeanor

evening falls
the beckons roll in quickly
the errors that unravel
well, they look like human faults
just like the energy she'd claim
if she dare say
a single word at all

she's silently so sure
the song she's singing from her soul
could use some simple paint
as it was written plain in black
and it's surely almost faded
into nothing but the color that it lacks

as she rests against a canvas
she ponders all the life that she might add
knowing not so much about the strangers,
just the energy they have

and the group slowly disperses
the lights shut off,
at first she thought
maybe she should follow suit..
but as the quiet rose she knew
that waiting for the lot to clear was worth it..
though the image she created wasn't perfect. end.

Sanctuary

It's your existence that kept me on my feet
A journey can't begin if I refuse to see that street
but knowing where it sits on a map is good for me,
good enough at least,
now that I have a place to be..

Breathe that cardboard scent
that mixes well with sense..
A common ground of clashing sound
and colors to the edge

Like pebbles sitting on a ledge
awaiting wind to give them strength..
the leaves flow by and laugh at them
though the drifters don't look flat like them..
They sit and pick out weighted trends
and foolish stems, and sentiments
and pass good vibes between good friends
amid some rush that doesn't end. End.

Numerology

From the beginning we were nothing but trouble..
Our house of cards collapsed
and amid the piles of rubble
were photographs and memories
from wherever we had stumbled
.. and they were perfectly intact
where everything else we had crumbled.

Numerology spread out from all the places that we went
in a gorgeous sea of emotion
ranging from black to red..
I said so many times I'd never go back there again
But I could not believe,
in that debris,
I left my friend.

Though the past is the past
it can never be changed
we traveled together from dirt roads to graves
we ended up driving each other insane
but what a good friendship, we somehow saved

and they say, young love won't die
and I look at the energy with you and I
and all that we learned from all that we tried
and now I always feel you, under the same sky

between each rise and fall
and when I randomly find
that I look at the clock
and I add up the time
and I see that the numbers are just like seeing your eyes..

You are every creation
And every collapse
And every good memory I somehow still have

You are the rain that I love
And the smoke I exhale
And the lines in my skin
And the flowers I fail

You're the number of times that I should have cared
And the sum of the answers that I never shared

You are the stolen, the found, and the viciously stoned,
And I am sorry, my dear, that I stopped coming home. End.

Repetition

For all of these years
we have lived on repeat
the same song and dance
with over-played themes..
we cannot connect our mismatched dreams
but we stay afloat in melodious streams..

And in the end, the music stops..
and the silence kills us both..
So we just rewind like we never left
coming in on a different note..

We've been singing and humming
and doing our thing
since so long ago..
but this track skips so often
it's so hard to take it slow..

Your words and my words
create a poetic verse,
a misleading sound
and a bittersweet curse..
We get lost in our rhythm
and go to town in our hearse..
and some days I wonder,
who was the worst?
Which one of us fell for the other one first?
Then how'd we get tangled so far from this earth?

Our energy is real, but the inertia hurts
as the radio hits a wall
and our speakers burst. End.

Fringe Benefits

We have frayed ends
that chaotically depend
on being linked to threads..
intertwined
combined
mislead..
Beneficial ties instead
of fringes lacking good intent..
We do our best to not forget
the base from which those fringes stem..

There's an unmistaken shift in trends
as he holds me and my heart defends
the concept of each plastic pen..
and the cap that comes with all of them. End.

Assistance

I just need a place to sit
I can be quiet,
I can help you out in silence
and I'm good for harsh reminders..
it's just that all of my consistencies seem to have retired
and I found myself rewired to a riot in crossfire

And I've never been a liar
though my words are loosely guided
as I settle with loose ties
when I'm hell bent on switching sides..

You told me how to stand cold and I handled it just right
I said the words that mattered,
balanced, sturdy, and polite..
and I really let him have it as I'd rather not to hide
but now I feel I'm in rare form
and I could use a drive..

And the road, it calls my name so much louder than a voice
.. and any other calls my way are cast into a void,
I roll the windows down to listen to the calming noise
and let the winter wind allow I make a colder choice

Then I'll meet you at the river
in my clothing from the street
and let you guide me to my seat
with overbearing chivalry..

I will try to keep it honest, but I'll tell you that you're sweet
and I will let you to my world
if you will tell me what you see. End.

Consistently Inconsistent

Be my secret
Be my lie
Be my reason..
Feed my spite
Be my high
and get me by..
Be the dagger in my side
Be the king of salty tides
and Sunday rides
and hollow vibes..
Won't you be my alibi
on the nights I need a place to hide?

Be my anger
Be my sigh
Be my muse
Be my third eye..
listen to the things I write
and share some lines
in songs you like..
Be the glow of fireflies
.. on and off on summer nights
My bittersweet roman-ticide..
.. on the rocks, with extra ice. End.

Sequere, Dux

I feel so blind
If you'd just let me flee
And let me find my own way free..

I do believe
that every key
has been created for a reason
and mine had meaning that I witnessed
on the evening I retrieved it..
how relieving it had been
to talk with someone
harshly speaking
but I pride myself on leaving
when the time is clear to me

Don't follow me
and please don't call me on the road
I have never feared what I don't know
and even bound I hang alone
I don't waste time on counting crows
and keeping track
of heart attacks
like that daft fool lost counting stars..
you are the aim that comes with arms
and turned a target for such harm
and all these words inside my blood
tearing my skin apart

I told you I'm a drifter,
and if forewarned is still forearmed,
you should have known I could fold quickly,
regardless of my cards..

---

and you taught me what I know
but now you stand there so alarmed
.. if you know me like you say then why is this so fucking hard?

What a good run
.. you could call it getting fucked
I am not above abrasive
.. if you're feeling extra tough
Conceal your whiskey
.. but be sure to drink it up
Then dive into that yellow dust,
I hope it falls and looks like us
..like what's left on the table isn't possibly enough. End.

Darling

Darling, take me in your arms
and pull me towards your heart..
twist my soul with your bare hands
and rip my mind apart..

You don't read my mind,
you feel my weakness in your core..
You've outsmarted me of course
But I am smarter than before..

I won't play your songs
so you're content to sit alone..
Living in those lyrics you resent
are not your own..
Call me when you're lonely
as my soul is for your taking..
It's important for the night,
but has our time been this forsaken?

You're convincing me
this mystery of what we could be
is worth all that sleep..
and those precious dreams,
that fell away
when I found defeat and misery..

But my heart has grown tired
Each tattered piece
I allowed to relax
in the dirt at your feet

I know you're a mess..
.. I'm just lost in your head
And lost in the darkness
of the sheets on your bed..
As we roll across eggshells
and silence regret
and we settle for such
as we're nothing instead. End.

Dear Guitarist

Dear Guitarist,
let me write you something honest..
and I swear it's from the ink out of my heart
I stare at this freshly painted apartment
.. another canvas I gave a false start

I may not always fathom of the farthest
and my everyday facade is not alarming
though I've battled with my mind
on how to gently warn you
that I'm just a hungry artist
with nothing but a poem for a target

You see,
I was starving for your muse
when I first heard you play guitar
and I hoped you'd pull those strings
to give me something good
that I might bring with me when I climb back in my car
and start back up the street
and eventually head back into my poorly lit apartment
where I'll fumble through my pages
and I'll stumble while I'm pacing
and I'll murmur to myself about the day,
for this, I'll thank you

Because I'm not above falling in love
and I'm not below bright thinking
I live farther than you can believe
and I'm drenched in my own ink. End.

I Give In

I give in..
I'm too exhausted
like you wanted,
I stopped thinking I could win..
And the thought of
fighting longer
is a daunting one to think..
I've held my own,
but man, I smoke
too much for this shit..
and you have my throat
even though
I told you
I give in. End.

Logic

It's been hundreds of months
and I've not wondered once
if our love is enough
as we laid our road rough..
We've called it bad luck
and we've called in corrupt
but this riddled road couldn't zigzag too much..

We're no more corrupt than the rest of the world
and no less in love
than the lies some endure..
but that fact of the matter is dependency hurts
and we refuse to fall victim to that vicious curse. End.

Carpentry

He offers his angry service
I remember it being worthless
He never made me nervous..
.. and that'd hurt him if he heard this…
But my heart turned out to be
something he couldn't burn
so he found himself a client
that wouldn't speak a word..
and when she finally runs away
I hope she finds a place to hide..
While he smokes a pack of butts
and waits impatiently outside..
He'll leave the empty package
So it sinks into her mind..
I stepped right on that trash
and didn't even bat an eye..
but she may not be so lucky
to put his sins into her rhymes
let them go in ink
to help her read between the lines..
Write him off before sunrise
take a drive
Don't buy those lies..
His business is the darker kind
with a contract made to bind a mind
and the skin it's in
with painful ties. End.

The Show Must Go On

I'll drop by
about a quarter after midnight
and pray that I can make you smile
and it might stick this time
Its fifteen miles
to the place that you'd take me each week
on the day that we always believed
was the reason we possessed those keys
and a map I said we shouldn't need..
Though it was such an easy read..

Tonight I'll leave a note
I'll make it some unfinished rhyme
I thought up on the road..

Our time unfolds..

Our clothes fall cold along the floor
to settle with my heart once more
I've settled here before
and I'm not sure
That amid the wars
and Sunday rides
and all those fights
and laughs
and lies..
we'd have built an honest enterprise
as uncertainty rests in your eyes..

A play like ours takes time to write
A stage so skewed..
and we act despite

---

the night
we fell through center stage
and couldn't improvise a word to say..
We both sighed without sound
trapped in the light
with our lies streaming down
and an audience of peers we knew nothing about
with their judgmental minds
routed straight to this town..

But we climbed back on stage
to resume our dead play
You had lines in your mind
that you could have rephrased..
but I just walked away
took a step to the left..
allowed the curtain to close
so I could finally rest
and that first breath I took
inspired me enough to add to a book
a journal of words from the curse that I shook..
That stare on your face
is just how you look..

And I can't be blamed
for the feeling you lost
You are acting as though
you somehow forgot..
All that we are, is too, all that we're not..
but we gave those poor characters
a nice honest shot. End.

Devil's Advocate

Shall I test your point of view, Doll?
Shall I lie in bed with you?
And convince you of off-truths..
like off-whitely painted rooms?
Pure.. yet stained
subdued..
subjected and assumed..
Surely those eggshells pass right through
imaginary shoes. End.

Options (2010)

We all have options..
we go with the flow
or we stand up and stop it..
commit to indolence
or die off exhausted
If you had to choose,
which would you want?

And your timeline can read
just as if you were strict
and so gently discreet
and contained in your script
and remained on the street
that continues from "Straight" to "Narrow" quickly..

Or maybe you're on a ship
that has long sailed away
from the docks
from the land
from your place in the sand
out of view from the bay that would always demand
that the line you'd create
disappeared with each wave
while you'd shift where you'd sit
just a bit
every day

The drifters, they fostered
a ship so exotic
a canvas so caustic
when all I had wanted
was gold in their future's from whoever "god" is
or however they'd name what they held in their pockets..

My hope was they'd hold
to an ethic so honest
with constant pursuance of gaining new knowledge..
Come through my doorway
when you're feeling lost and
I'll show you what they'll never teach you in college. End.

My Verse, No Bridge

I don't question why
nobody stands at my side..
between my frosted heart
and nonsensical pride..
but I don't have the time
to keep saying good-bye..
I never cared because you never tried..
Now I'm stuck in a box
while you wave from outside
saying you miss me but that's just a line
You're so intelligent
that I thought you'd be sly..
There's no one else on this earth
that could finish your rhymes..
I gave this up to you,
though I knew it was mine..
We could try
but you and I would never be fine..
There was a time
You could understand my side
but now you barely understand your own
God damn life..
What a surprise.. you think our connection just died..
but you killed us off
just like the rest of the times
and I can't just rewind..
That beat wasn't right..
My heart was already cold,
now it's entirely ice..
So, you can sit back
and take a look at our lives
and maybe one of these days
you will want to know why. End.

Demolition

Your water destroys the image I'm creating with my paint
but my heart is beating faster than the clouds can pour the
rain..
You stand there staring at me
and you almost look amazed..
your eyes, they tell me more than that blank look upon your
face..
concrete and grey..
but your eyes are mostly blue,
with a touch of dark untruth
and a twisted point of view..
... a kaleidoscope...
we collide in music notes
I'll paint them on our walls
so when they fall
our song might flow..
We didn't know,
we had it all along,
we just arranged the music wrong
it might have been a lovely song
had it not crumbled with those walls we said were strong. End.

Revenge

My revenge was inspired
by the luck of the Irish
and each fucking time
he said he loved fires...
He says he's retired..
.. real carpentry now..
wired with jewelry
and roaming around..
And he only sees
the world at his feet
when he's laying floor beams
back where they should be..
All the while forcing me onto my knees
on a loft he insisted
he built just for me..
He handles my heart
how he handles his speech..
.."verbal mistakes.." he says ignorantly..
and his words rattled free
like the tools in his Jeep
and they'd silence the sound of me
trying to speak..
but I had faith in those flammable leaves,
and his damaging creed..
and the trees he'd strut over
with joyous defeat..
I knew they'd catch faster
with gasoline..
but the reaction meant more
with a flame burning free. End.

Hey Man

Hey man, do you have some bud?
I'm all out of luck.. I just have a few bucks..
You can have that
along with my trust,
and my excuse for a heart I will tell you is corrupt..
Uncover my rust
while you brush off my dust
and assure me that you don't believe in real love,
but you'd like to leave
maybe get on a bus..
and discover a town that doesn't know us..

You know what, man?
Sounds like a plan..
It's time we abandon this outlandish land
that we over-discovered
from the sticks to the sands..
I'll walk with you but don't hold my hand. End.

Wrong Place, Right Time

Am I lacking good sense?
Shall I tear down this fence?
Build a brick wall instead?
Climb to the top and look down from the ledge?
.. they won't say I don't live my life on the edge..

What do I have but a year I regret,
while lost in the ink of an unfortunate pen?
I can't tell you again..
I take that back, I won't say this again
I've considered it said..
As my secrets seep through the cracks in the cement..

My foundation destroyed
all for time spent employed
by a man in a suit
that drives, and thinks, in main routes..
He hated the truth
and I would have just withered if not for abuse
or the shoes that I wore
on my day of recruit. End.

Rise Above It

My love some days is so afraid
ashamed of all those chains we made..
He hates me for those changes made..
but I'm the same
so he can't complain..

He fakes up rage and knows I'll wait
though he loves the way I run away..
He pushes 'til his pencil breaks
and decides the page is all mistakes..

If only I could read his face
but nowadays it all looks fake..
Just like the words he used to say
on the nights that he'd keep me awake
with promises he couldn't make
and dreams that I just couldn't shake. End.

Hidden Personal Realizations

I'd rather be empty
than filled with lost purpose
and stitched to the side
of a quilt I deemed worthless..
And I wasn't fabricated until a thread surfaced,
that lead me to question
the way that my shirt fit..

A version of life I had grown to deny..
An aversion to why
I was hell-bent to hide..
and I lied
when I told them I wasn't afraid
because facing those fears
is how courage is made..
Though denial is never the same as escape
so I took a trip
and I tried to pray..

I remember the day
I first walked by the church
covered in dirt
with my mind on my shirt..
I thought,
'what could it hurt?'
find a minister..
and tell him the ways that my body was cursed..'

The doors opened up..
an angel inside,
reminding me of the times I had the sun on my side..
I wondered of light
and how well she could fight..

then looked at my life, before stepping inside..
but I was instantly swallowed by my need to walk out
and the block in my mouth said I should have gone south
to reside with the hippies
and give up on doubt..
I could have had friends, but I do well without..

A cloud of smoke eased my mind..
I knew that my journey was just as divine
as the peace I could find
If I gave the lord time..
So I gave up on thread
and re-stitched up with twine
and some rhymes
when I took to the lines
and wrote about grief
and old linens of crime
and you wouldn't believe
the relief in release
unless you took a trip to find new energy
and you stumbled on answers you wouldn't have seen,
had you believed in religion
before destiny
or left your muse at home
when you went westerly. End.

Our Little Talks

"You look like Monday mornings"
"You look like Sunday nights"
"You look like you come with warnings, babe"
"You're one giant warning sign.."
"You look like a music note mixed in with useless rhymes"
"And you look like a writer that has wasted too much time.."
"You look like you never tried to keep your pen from running
dry"
"Well.. you look really high..
.."

"..I feel like you must love me.."
"I feel you must be wrong,
I feel like I've denied myself
those feelings for too long.."
"They must be gone.."

As time ticks on..

"You look more broken than before"
"And you look like
my heart, alive
and walking out the door.."
"Darling, of course..
you look so harmless when you're sleeping"
"And you look like
I love you enough
that this is almost worth me keeping"
"I feel so weakened"
"Are you thirsty from this heat?
You look like you lack energy.."
"You look like you lack synergy
and mystery

and chivalry
my bittersweet bad company.."
"You look just like that change I need"
"You're the wave that knocks me off my feet..
Shall I say a prayer whilst on my knees?
You look so far away from me.."
"You're reveries tear at my seams
as if my heart could stand to speak..
you're words are harsh
and bleak in beat.."
"But babe, you wrote that beat for me.."
"I can't write what I can't see"
"Your love must be pure subtlety.."
"Like a puddle that's six inches deep..
..but I still believe my mind can dream,
and you're the Sunday I can get some sleep.."
"You're every day of every week."   End.

Change in Pace

The lyricist takes to the sea..
you best believe
his anchor drags,
his vessel slacks,
the current flows by,
he sits down to relax..
He takes a seat
hidden somewhere in back
and invites you to see
all the music he has..

It is beautifully sad..
Imagine a life that is reduced to a fad..
The fifteen-year-olds scream when he plays his old tracks
and he's looking at me
like he expects I'll do that..
But I take out a pen
and I write on his pad
and he stares at my soul
as if he'd like to ask
if I had gone mad
and my soul gently laughs
as I copy down words
I felt the lines lacked..

He didn't expect I'd have words in my chest
and he wouldn't have guessed
I could write with the best..
But regardless of jest
or the zest of a mess,
he allowed his poor pen to a terrible death..

Now he escapes to the sea
to escape from the stress
of the rest of the world
and the secrets he's kept..
But I rock his boat with the extents of my depth
and it fucks with his world
omitting relent..
And I know he regrets that extra few cents..
And the album he gave me..
.. just a vacant remnant
of the time that we spent
that I grew to resent..
He wants me off his ship he so proudly pretends..

I walk the plank,
I can't wait for the blue..
or the view of his ship
while it continues to move
farther away from his old passing dreams..
He'll take a seat
I know he'll think of me..
He'll read my words when he's alone in the sea
and resent the fact that he let me float free. End.

Art of Fact

The wet paint upon broken glass
holds it intact..
The art of fact..
.. poor artifact
barely valued for real cash
but is there really shame in that?

The colors connect
and they respect
what they protect..
That canvas that allowed them life..
The space a piece needs to survive..

Without a set place on this earth
ideas disappear as quickly as words..
And a picture is worth a thousand for sure..
..though a penny for my two cents
seems so absurd..
Take that ten bucks
and call it good luck,
while I get on a bus and leave this block in the dust..
This mile of route
hurts less than the truth..
What's a nice honest walk
between me and you?
Could we share some time?
Could I share some rhymes,
while you tell me the lines in the music you like?
Babe, can't you write?
Or at least touch the tide?
I'll paint with any color that shows it's alright..

I've painted the cracks,
and I've hated, in fact..
but you can't say that glass
always lasts
this far passed
the foundation of staff
that can look back
and laugh
at the plaque that I use
as a platform for tact..
..so there's no art in fact..
but somehow it takes so much work just to have..
It follows so closely to questions we ask,
but somehow
some minds
can't be wrapped around that. End.

Who Made Who?

Who taught who to be a soldier?
Who taught who to climb a cliff?
Who showed who the power of a leader
.. with that balance and those calloused fingertips?

Who trusted you to shift your fate?
And offered you a good, solid home base?

So focused on your present,
who accepted you and promised a blank slate?
..so your future could be made
.. so I could sing your praises
and hopefully one day you'd have enough to finally say
that you are ready for a change..

So, who taught who to lead the way?
Who walked me through the process?
Who was there for my mistakes?
and who was really honest?
Possibly a lyricist, a few misplaced guitarists
plumbers, truckers, carpenters
and many different artists

All of whom had merely
but a single thing in common,
not their stories or their colors,
but their aptitude for knowledge. End.

Changes

The first words he spoke I'd never heard..
descriptively,
cryptically,
expressive with his verbs..
and I had yet to encounter
something on this earth
that could reduce my heart to dirt..
.. simply a stain upon my shirt..
a timely curse..

And as the time ticks on
so many wrongs
will only work
when we are the ones who write the laws..
I'm always right
He knows he's always right..

We both lied
quite a few times..
And staggered on purely for spite..
We'd feel the love
within our tide
on our own time..
And that first night we closed our eyes,
opened our minds,
and defensive lines..
Though my darling just prefers to hide..
He still denies this curse of rhyme
I believed his heart was worse than mine
and down the line
He proved me right..

But I had faith in failing light
A failing flame..
.. at times untamed..
somehow unnamed
remained sustained..

But he won't speak of our old days,
he communicates a different way..
He doesn't have unbroken chains,
he'll save some pieces when they break..
displayed in vain,
riddled with shame..
A disarray..
..as if that changed. End.

Rant of Pride

When there is nothing between us
don't imagine my face..
Keep closing your eyes
to a dreamless sleep state
I won't suffocate
and I can't orchestrate
a band large enough
to play the sound of our fate..
.. symphony of blaze..
They called it a phase,
but that fire burned longer
than an arsonist's rage..
Spent nearly six years now
living in flames,
I have third degree stains,
I'm so far passed pain..
And I'm done playing games
I am done fielding blame..
You always open your mouth
right when I walk away,
and our fate is my fault
because I didn't wait..
What a tiresome way
to handle my days. End.

Darling, Two

Darling, give me a week of space
to dry the fresh ink that I've placed..
I've never been one to showcase
the effects of that look on your face..

Each iris leads straight to your core
where we stand hand-in-hand at a shore..
And the tide slowly climbs to our feet
leaving a line of such desperate defeat..
And I urge you to walk towards the waves
but you prefer solid earth,
where it's safe..

As the sun slowly sets on the scene,
and more land is consumed by the sea,
you back off..
..it's like watching you leave
anytime your eyes cut into me. End.

Nailbiter

He showed me a love
doused in grey lonesome dove..
Could look good polished up
though my nerves make it tough..
And it's never enough
to live through the sunrise
and still see the sunset when I look in his eyes..
His breath gets me high
and for a moment in time we both almost smile..
but our eyes remain locked
and I can't pull away
I can't make it stop..
But I can't make me stay..
I almost forgot that I drown in these waves
I flounder at best
when I see his face. End.

Guilty Pleasures

I get caught in the waves..
I'm ashamed to admit
that my soul can't refrain
from the comfort of pillows that fall to my face
and marijuana smoke that stands still in its place..
..but I digress
because any circumstance
in reality is a mess,
so why not accept the parts that make
the least amount of sense? End.

Short Story

I once believed I needed words to add to my foolish rhymes,
a way to finish out my thoughts
because I was unsatisfied..
So I asked the washed out lyricist to dock and help me write
but he hadn't touched a pen in years..
.. my request was denied
I kept filling in my words
with hope that I might find
something similar to his pad
or the patterns in his time..
The lyricist then beckoned for a pen on a new day..
He told the same old stories
but those details must have changed..
When I urged his pen to write the words down anyway
he told me he's all out of words..
.. and I'm the one he blames..
I had no idea that these were something I could take..
And all his good ideas, I guess, had rinsed off in the waves..
So he took me to the docks and asked if I was feeling brave,
and before I could say anything,
he stabbed me and I sank. End.

Silver Bullet

A speeding silver bullet
reminiscent of your fingertips
I take deep breaths and count to five
before I take that hit..

Your words feel fake
just like your touch..
Have half a mind
to give us up..
The other half
stuck in the past
glued to time that had to pass..
I stare at you through shattered glass
and count the cracks
in case you ask..
useless knowledge of the facts
amassed like trash in plastic bags..
I stash red flags I have out back
I found they filled my closet fast..
I pulled them up along our path
'cause looking at them makes me laugh
with you I cut myself in half..
Because of this I can't relax..

We're five years weak..
.. I did the math
and looking back
I look quite daft..
I never thought time moved this fast
but we know the end for thoughts like that..
.. she fell for wrong
and it collapsed
along with the ideas they had..

This sounds like how we almost match,
but I'm not like you..
.. for this, I'm glad..
My heart's a lock
yours is a latch..
My pieces don't come unattached..
Yours come apart as separate halves
and I can't be the lock you lack. End.

Common Law

On day three sixty five
of a love so denied
I kissed you good-bye
and moved on with my life..
You close your eyes,
it's like I'm by your side..
You hold somebody's hand
but you know it's not mine..

You know there was a time
we were two yellow lines,
like a canvas for ink
that ran miles and miles..
Our consistency broke
and now we just collide..
We got so backed up
we installed a stop sign
that eventually turned to a full traffic light
We'd occasionally run
out of spite
for delight. End.

My Bittersweet

You are the lover in my dreams
my most amazing reveries
though I am only really pleased
when you are with me when I sleep..
.. my bittersweet. End.

Tis the Season

I'm following the sun around the yard
keeping from the shadows used to seem so hard..
but lately I've been craving sun
evading where the shade has come..
The warmth, it melts away my numb
and loosens up my tongue..
that damn noose that I had hung
still dangles neat and freely from
a place that never sees the sun..
and they never saw it coming
when I saw it best to run
because I didn't want to die
inside of walls that grew to hide my life
and suffocate me with false pride
like I was really safe inside..
.. damn that foolish guard of mine..
Welcome back
my darling lie..
Remind me why you're so unkind..
Open up my tired eyes
and ask me for this light of mine. End.

Seating

All my words
these meaningless words
worthlessly placed
in patterns I've heard..
as if I've earned the right
to return to the verbs
and grammatical errors
like I never learned..

And I notice those changes
your person enables..
riddled with doubt
ornamenting our table..
And we face each other
.. so willing and able
reclining
unwinding
reliant on angles
in the centerpiece
in between comfortable strangers..
I'm sorry my dear,
but you aren't an angel
and this broken vase is
just far too entangled
with vines that are trying
to strangle my patience..

This painless arrangement
adds weight to the table
heavy enough that the surface is breaking..
with too much distraction
to keep up conversation..

Our spatial relation is becoming invasive..
Am I being too vague?
Or am I being abrasive?
A screen holds more water
than this god damn vase is..
Stop tracing each crack
like you're gonna erase..

Let's face it
our placement
could use extra spacing. End.

Completion

I removed a window pane
to create a masterpiece..
The glass was always beautiful
but it lacked a destiny..
The spectrum looked as radiant
as any pain could be..
So why not allow the world a piece of pure *aestheticy*?

I never thought I'd walk along this artwork with bare feet..
Ignoring all the damage
regardless of how deep..
The numbness sweeps me up sometimes
and I almost believe
that the glass I have been walking on has not once made me
bleed..

I'm not bitter toward the space
that my dear canvas had to leave
It's been a cold December but I lost heat I didn't need..
And I don't regret the DNA left on each broken piece
as my artistic downfall lies precisely in those genes..

But this has been an open project
I've been desperate to complete
and I found a shift in vision
is not necessarily defeat..
From a martyr to a mason,
Now I proudly take a seat
and stare blankly at the wall
where that old window used to be. End.

Aestheticy is not a word recognized by any dictionary I found

---

Genesis: A Story

We're the worst love story written,
the most confusion ever read..
And we're the words between those lines
from the beginning to the end..
We are fragile,
paper-thin,
and riddled with amends..
A paperback abridgement,
crippled and pretend..
We are the Spark Notes of a novel
passed between two friends
that even after skimming
they don't know what the author said..
We are a book worth burning
with our bridge and bad intent
as we go our separate ways to know
we'll never speak again..
I'll write a brand new story
to the tune of the cement..
then you can read my words and know
you couldn't touch this pen. End.

On the Road Tune

You can find me on the road
You can feel me in the wind
You can say I'm a mess
and you hate how I dress
but you miss me again..

You can see me in the trees
When the breeze is strong
You can sing me in a song
Could you sing me in a song?

You can feel me in the waves
if you dare to face the blue
You can write me off in ink
knowing every single ship
reminds me of you

You can read me in the notes
in all the lyrics that I wrote
and when you think that you know
but it turns out you don't..
You can find me on the road. End.

Credit (remix)

Yeah, I can make beats
and I can tear seams
and I can one-two-step around railroad beams..
And I could write a rap
that would include some history..
and let it be the mystery
of who the hell gave this to me..

I fill in the blanks
in the lines on the street..
and I rock with the words
that appear at my feet..
And I run a tight shift,
you know how it is..
high as a kite
with some extra uplift..
I got something to prove
and hard work isn't it..
It's that working hard
isn't as hard as you think..

So I built up these bricks
and conducted business
to flow like the smoke..
.. enticing and vivid..
A timid young vision
addicted to wishing
and building beginnings
from my lonely prison..
..you fit in
with all of your unwashed wishes..
You fixed into all my most rigid of ridges
whistling on with all of my bridges

and adding in words
when I couldn't finish..

But sit down and listen
to the tune in the walls..
They'll be singing long after
the drifters are gone..
And someone will be there
humming along
without knowing who wrote
the words to the song. End.

Click

Call me crazy
but I'm jumping off this train..
If not, I'll hit the same place
and I'd really be insane
because it's not as though
this railroad's destination is gonna change..
I knew where this was headed
and I boarded anyway..
.. a sound escape..
Just to avoid a little rain?
I'm so drenched I can't be drained..
and what's another grey cloud
when the water's all the same?
I can't complain..
'Cause lately I've been testing sound
and frankly,
I'm just guessing now
expressing doubt
repressing nouns I know too well
to write them down. End.

One Sick Motherfucker

The author draws in charcoal white,
Human eyes personify a canvas left blank otherwise..
..he's one of those creative minds..

He has a dream
a storyline,
with ideas of the novel kind..
He writes just like he draws his lines,
from the basement of the Grand Design..

He's underground but sits so high..
Amazed and gazing at sunlight..
One day he'll surely see the sky
or at least get close enough to lie. End.

Anklet

I'm the broken fin of a dolphin
hanging from a string..
Tied to my own company, I'm out here on a limb..

As I dangle near the ground
I shall embrace the mess I'm in,
all the while knowing I'm a symbol for my sins

Saint Christopher can't save me
from the dirt or from the wind,
he merely holds the faith that will
protect the way I live..
Staring at this piece I am,
this broken strung-up fin, all I can think..
is at least this knotted line assures me
gravity can't win. End.

Abstract Noun

It is almost like
I vividly
remember when
my heart was clean
but see the difference
in the scenes
and understand
what difference means. End

Jab

Old friend
I'll never return
I have no concern
for bridges I'd written
on pages I've burned..
Say that I'm wicked
like it really hurts
and revert back to verses
you can't claim as yours..

Bury your journals down into the dirt
and one day erosion will leave them unearthed
You'll assuredly stagger
and trip on your words..
and that will hurt worse
than my threatening verbs. End.

Johnny Holland

He calls himself grateful
while he's on the road
and he sends that vibe out
to the drifters back home

He knows that we care
'cause when he was alone
we appeared at his side
in a line..
.. the way we always rolled

He had called us all out
without evening knowing
and as sure as our flow
we responded in note

And I hope that he holds
his mortality close
and carries a map
wherever he goes. End.

Be the Leaf

Catch a break
Catch a breeze
Catch the wind
and be that leaf..
From here on out
I know no ground..
This shift in wind
is where I'm bound. End.

Guilt-ridden Inspiration

I want to pray to my muse
and beg for forgiveness,
And say so sincerely
that I'm sorry for sinning
..and singing..
and writing my words
based on a curse
that my muse could have cured..

But what's worse
is I allowed my energy to come from a soul
so entirely cold
empowered by folds
in a journal he sold
for twice the price it was purchased for
as if his touch simply made it
worth that much more..
And I was drawn to the lines
unaware that each crease was so easily torn..
..am I this easily scorned?
I didn't realize my heart could conform
to adorn a sleeve
so regularly worn..

And I scramble for speech
as I struggle to read
the words that the wind has allowed me to see..
I'd love a reprieve
I pray for relief..
I just wish that my muse would take over for me. End.

Body Language Forced

I put my hands inside my pockets
to make me feel more passive,
Is it awful that my feelings are really that elastic?

I can stand at ease
in pure appeasement
without asking
for a reason
in my stance of real well-seasoned satisfaction..

And awareness might make up
for a small fraction of disaster
though it will never compensate
for all the weight I didn't factor

Staring straight was all that mattered
now I'm famous for these patterns
and my aim shows great improvement
so I'll use it while I have it. End.

Courage Beads

My feet connect to ground like they're magnetic for a second
I've been walking since November
and the pavement sounds like severance..
I remember how it felt
before my gypsy string untethered..
..like I never had the courage,
I just kept the beads together

And Saint Christopher can't measure up
or better this protection,
or the lessons that I learned
when it was time my weight should lessen,
I should make a straight confession
even though it seems possessive..
I saved one of my courage beads for personal reflection. End.

My Sister's Beads

Those gypsy beads
won't bring you peace
unless the string breaks naturally..
I should have told you what it means
to wear an anklet you can't keep

You looked like you could use the green..
I hoped once it broke you might break free..
Instead it led you to believe
that broken hopes attach to me. End.

Mother Dearest

Mother Dearest, am I just another seashell?
One that used to live beside the rest?
Floating
Flowing
Knowing
Growing..
Deep within the depths..
So blind to shifting swells, that couldn't move me yet..
And then one day I felt a shift
so powerful I fell to it
and drifted to a place I couldn't tell you made much sense..

Mother Dearest,
am I simply a dark rose?
One withered from faults purely of my own?
Put in a nice vase..
.. a quaint resting place
like I ruined my chances to grow on the day
I decided 'twas time to move towards a change
from the roots that which gave me my thorns
and the truth that created my need to escape..
.. and I still swore I knew even more the next day..

But pride turned to faith
that surely looked fake..
it's a much drier life
now that I'm in the vase..
The longer I'm here, the faster it drains
and it feels like the faucet gets farther away..
Though I'm not as exhausted as many could say
'cause I haven't forgotten
how I got this way..

But honestly, Mother
I'd just like some water..
It's getting much harder to find everyday..
I'm here for the journey
and learning to worry
and praying my vase doesn't break on the way..

Am I plagued by a fate
'cause I sunk into pages,
ignoring the faces
of those that embraced
a true dream they could chase
while I just want hydration?
Give me a sign that I'm not going crazy
I feel like I'm fading
I'm losing my patience..
I fear finding out what I'm really afraid of..
..but now that I'm here I can see what I'm made of..
'Cause you didn't make up
the fate behind Thought..
.. or the weight of the rocks that she found chasing Wrong..
Mom, do I even still look like your daughter?
If not, would you say that I'm not too far off? End.

You Can't Take It With You

I take two cardboard boxes
that are duct-taped at the seams..
It seems I've owned more dust
than anything to keep..
I go to pack my things
and the thunder turns to speak..
It reaches down into a box
and hands a book to me..
"Don't forget your bible,
it's the most important piece"
"Piece of shit," I said in jest..
.. he stood up violently,
"Piece of you, piece of this, of all the ink you bleed.."
"But I'll always have a pen, " I said,
"and something good to read."
"Won't you take it with you?
This book showed you how to be.."
"That isn't really how it works,
it stays here when I leave." End.

You Know What Happened to Thought?

The sun did rise
and take her faith
the whole up.

She washed her face,
and combed her bangs,
boarded the train,
like there was nothing to give up..

like it was nothing to give up on harsh remembering.
Or the burning embers she once swore she couldn't feel
that now resemble tiny marks
which are inarguably real.

She was starving for new diction,
New additions.. and grammatical nutrition..
a different type of rhythm
and a refined way of thinking.

She was Thought
enlightened purely,
she was shockingly more curious
than any chance to learn
she'd ever lived or laughed before.

And she drags her smoke a little hot
wishing she'd forgotten all those moments
that she swore she had left lost within the fog.

Eleven years of writing on,
rewinding songs, and fighting dawn..
Light finally broke and cast upon
a ground that she could steady on..

.. and honestly if not for wrong,
if not for shedding colors
unessential to adventure
she could no longer prolong..
she might never have reverted
to a canvas she'd considered
to be wanness and imperfect..
though it was plain enough
that the color in her person
finally surfaced.

She always knew it would be worth it..
wander strong enough to prove
the deep set litany of learning on a paved road
couldn't cure her pen of unrest or ambiguity
she understood ambitiously
until the thought occurred to breathe
And now that Thought's referred to as a
pure Epiphany. End.

Wildflower

A soul feeling wild blew a wish to the wind
and inspired creation to drift
light and thin,
Painting the world to a visible shift
that settles when science insists it to sit..

A journey inside each piece of this wish
that is fixed to the truth
we all live to exist..

And in time each seed
turned into a weed
that blossomed the sun
on a stem of pure green,
But one drifted free
and that dandelion stood out amidst all the trees..

Stitched into the seams
where the grass meets the leaves
it established itself
on a pathway that leads
away from the east..
.. where the sunlight retreats
just beyond the horizon
it will find what it needs. End.

Hope

Maybe
the road
will save me,
who knows?
And take me to those
who make
their own hope..
Head toward the west coast..
Build a new home..
See the sunrise
from someplace
I don't know.   End.

Nevada and Colorado

Let me call upon my muse
and move quickly from the sea..
Send my signals to the air
and hope to catch a breeze

Witnesses will tell you
that I've worked my life away,
swimming toward the shore
but I refuse to kneel to pray

And as the sun was rising
a year ago today
I was walking down the road
with a suitcase and some change
calling on my angels
who would promise me good grace
but receiving empty letters
from a vessel far away

He pushed the envelope my way
with a postmark and my name..
But the stamp was worth much more
before the mailman came..
And now I have these words
that he felt so inclined to say,
in ink that never dried
leaving my fingers lightly stained

So everything I touch now
just reminds me of the day
I decided he
inspired me
enough to leave the bay. End.

Dandelion

I cannot sleep
I can't stop dreaming of the weed
that journeyed so far from the east
and over rocks
and roads
and streams..
Through all those cities we once deemed
too far away for us to reach..

Limitlessly flowing free..
so unlike old redundant beats
that circled feats and mockery
in albums under lock and key
designed by animosity

But this dandelion fostered flee..
It is how his soul first got to me..
and haunted me
and taunted me
to fall in love
so honestly. End.

Rocky Mountain High

I fought for so long
to deny myself love,
repainting the shards
that I found in my blood..
I had saved them as gifts
from the sea..
..so corrupt
But eventually I couldn't hide from the doves
that would carry my heart across land
like the bus
that I took
when I got my first look at you, Love. End.

Amarillo

I burst in rushed and heavy
and I steady out my voice
announcing my new presence
and the tenant wanders out as though my entrance was
expected..

Familiar as the energy about him
(masked by a blank face)
was a look that I mistook as my reflection
so I stared for just a second
and I swear he read my mind that day
(he swears he was just guessing)

But he gathered up a remedy
to balance out my energy
suggesting that the mess of me
I carried through his door weighed less already

So I confessed my stress did shift
and recklessly I did admit
that I felt just a bit misfit
standing there so fixed on petty anger
So I digressed before regret
of daftly words I could have meant
and he allowed that I pretend
to do without an anchor

He handed me a little green container
insisting that my wager be
to change the weight I roll into each paper..

.. and instantly I recognized this stranger

You Know What Happened to Thought?

A Poetry Compilation

Meghan Victoria

And the contents
And the color
And the comfort of the cover
I am not ashamed to say I will lose later. End.

Dear Mary-kate

Life goes
and life goes wrong..
Our flow is interrupted
Some evil wind might force you roll corrupt
but suffer strong

Darling, you are not alone
regardless of where I might roam
I swear I'm sending all good vibes
I hope they make it where you call your home..

I think of you
when coffee brews
and sunlight forces its way through
the blinds
And I hold the wheel so awkwardly
and laugh out loud like you're with me
then catch a good glance at that empty seat
And wonder if you know you're on my mind

I think of where we've grown
and what we have grown into..
..all those trees and all that green
As slanted as the world might seem,
I wonder when we learned that seeds
don't always need to grow
where they are planted..
And extremes only exist so much as stress
when you can't help but sweat
where you have landed..

You Know What Happened to Thought?

A Poetry Compilation

Meghan Victoria

When all else fails
just be the leaf,
at times caught up within a breeze,
and when the winds seem to have eased,
enjoy ground level just as pleased..

And if that's where you sit
when I come walking up the street,
knowing me,
I'd see you and think, what a gracious leaf. End

Dirt

It is a long way down the dirt before the highway
and the road is washed out for miles in between
It looks like more dark clouds are heading my way
as the nightfall is encroaching on the seam..

Somehow shadows always tend to fill these gaps
to make up for whatever we might lack
And while we hide amidst them
we repress our inner missions.
and to anybody looking we are missing. End.

Chasing Thunder

I thought I'd write much more in Arizona
and being stuck on The Raton,
I could have sent a couple verses home

I thought I'd write a novel in Nevada
and possibly I'd publish
when I got to the ocean
but I forgot the thought
when I made it to the coast and watched
this tangent of a sunset fall
into infinity
while I stared so intently from my rock along the beach

And I thought the Golden Gate City
a pure poetic place where I could think
So sure I'd meet a classic muse
sip some coffee
spill some ink
and greet the ideas turning loose..
And creativity, well it rarely does evade me
..but in that San Francisco Bay, not a single verse escaped me

Like up by the Atlantic
in New Hampshire
while hand-washed clothes hung out to dry
in the humid, northeast summer shine
I could have felt more frantically inclined to sit and scribe
but every item I'd adorned
already sat so weighted on a line
and over-worn

And driving down that open road in Kansas..
Silently I sat, swapping out my threads,
sifting through my mind's diction
coming up with stanzas in my head..
.. I could have left them to a napkin
but I chose to keep them to myself instead

Much like going to Cheyenne and
enjoying every moment that my lips hit the ceramic
The frozen highway just outside my window
served a couple cautious cars
that were seemingly just idling through transit..
I watched life in slow motion
taking in the frigid winter dances of Wyoming
only lowering my cup
when the waitress offered that she'd fill it up. End.

Always Singing There

Where the sand meets with the water
and the interstate stops
Where the waves crash to the shore
and we sit safely on the rocks
Where the storm has come to calm itself
and the fog begins to lift
and the sun casts on each blade of grass
when our world finally shifts..

I'm where the pavement turns to dirt
and the road just disappears
Somewhere amidst the switchbacks
riding heavy on the gears
Some place between the east and west
set underneath the moon
where the rainfall comes to cool the earth every afternoon

I'll be in every map,
on every road,
in every song..
in our race toward the horizon,
toward infiniti and on..
I'll be somewhere in the breeze,
I'll be somewhere in the wind,
my lips against my coffee cup while my speakers sing..
Stopped some place down the road,
passed where the gypsies would reside,
and when you make it down the trail,
I'll see you on the other side. End.

You Could Make This Place Beautiful

I am in pieces
but I see you breathing

and your life.. well, it brings my life meaning

.. and nothing will take you away..

You look healthy and strong
and I've known you this long
this feels easy and natural
.. and nothing is wrong for today

You are rooting and blinking
and moving and thinking
how wild and weird the world seems
And darling, I promise
its normal and awkward
and life, well existence, ain't free
It will come at a cost
you will learn when you're lost
but for now you are safe here with me
I will share what I know
I will give what I own
and I'll pray that you grow
to a man who exists happily

I pictured these moments
for years, without knowing
the treasure in seeing your face
though I felt in my heart I'd known you all along
.. you'd been with me in some tiny trace

You Know What Happened to Thought?

A Poetry Compilation

Meghan Victoria

Our great human hearts
are not built without flaws
and I'll be there whenever yours breaks..
Life can get heavy and be hard to carry
but I'll help you train for the weight

There is nothing more sure and nothing more pure,
and nothing that brings me more faith
than my hope for your future
and how each moment with you here
is a moment that was well worth the wait. End.

Renaissance Man

I still know where to find you
It's almost like you never left
Time can't change where we laid you to rest

Down the same back roads
Just beyond the pond from all the stories that you told
Those stories, man, they never did get old

I still look for your belongings from the bridge over that pond
When the sun casts down just right upon the water
I swear I see your things along the bottom
But much like you, they're gone just not forgotten

And fairly often
I find myself driving down your routes
softly reminiscing of each time
that I had been down them with you
I can still hear the music
As if the album never stopped..
"We're Only in it for the Money" is still rolling through the songs

And I still seek out all those places when I'm lost

And I pull up to you when I feel the most defeated
..climb onto the old familiar stone
and puff most of a pack of smokes
right where I am seated
while I fill you in on life since our last meeting
(..as if you didn't see it)

They all said time would help with healing,
but it doesn't make it easier each day you aren't here
your absence is more normal,

though that doesn't change the weight
that I am feeling more with every fleeting year..

I miss you more with passing time
.. equated to learning to ride a bike..
you raised me to get on and go
well, Dad, I crash a lot, you know
I'm supposed to be improving but I'm barely up the road

But thanks to you I keep it moving
And thanks to you I get back up
.. thanks to you I struggle but I'm always strong enough..
and thanks to you I've floundered more than once
only to come to find
that I am fine
without a crutch

Just know that I remember who you were
deep in your heart
and know that I'm alright and that I never fell apart
And your legacy and memory are settled safely in your
grandson who is sleeping in my arms
I know he'll hold you in such high regards

So here you sit, guarded on the grounds of old Saint Stephen,
a martyr who was stoned to death
and now those stones, built like a wreath,
protect you where you rest

and I hate that you live here
But at least I know
that you are always here. End.

To The Moms Who Once Rode Trains:

Yes, you moms who once rode trains,
or trucks, or cars, or vans
and found your way across the land
with backpacks
or with rucksacks,
or with nothing but the layers on your back..
I have to ask..

Do you still have your rocks?
Did you keep your little trinkets from the places you had
stopped?
Do you keep them on your person or tucked in a treasure box?
Do you share them with your children or save them for your
thoughts?

And did you hang onto each ticket stub
you'd actually paid cash and
does that whistle give you goosebumps
while you're sitting there in traffic?
Do you show your children maps of where you traveled?
Do you show them photographs
or do you leave them to imagine?

Do you still dream of going back there?
Where all you'd need is a duffle bag
and some cigarettes
and a solid laugh
Where you'd fill your pockets with sugar packets
and never did you decline those matches
.. they're free
And that's the most "free" most of us had ever seen..

We would dream of those adventures
Even growing from misfortune on the way
We had been so lost and found at once
but grounded by the setting sun,
at the end of our rough days

And do you remember what it's like along the highway?
Can you recall when you'd awaken while light breaks?
Were you moved by the sun rising?
your next home on the horizon..
.. but you wouldn't be arriving
for another fifty miles

..moments likes those
made me feel the most alive

So to the transients,
and those gypsy folks,

and the travelers,

and the rolling stones,

to the nomads who never kept a home

And the lone rangers..

all you wandersome souls..

.. my cup is raised to your time on the road. End.

You Know What Happened to Thought?

A Poetry Compilation

Meghan Victoria

Cheers.

101